Win Your Texas Injury Case

David Todd, Attorney at Law

Legal disclaimer: I am not allowed to give legal
advice in this book. The suggestions and the
warnings I provide in this book are not a substitute
for consulting with or hiring an attorney. Please
remember that I cannot give you legal advice unless
and until you hire me and I have agreed in writing
to accept your case.

Introduction

If you or someone you care about has recently been injured in an accident, you are probably feeling a number of different emotions: fear, frustration, anger, worry, or just plain confusion. You are probably unsure how to proceed.

You may be wondering: will my insurance company treat me fairly? Will the other person's insurance company treat me fairly? Will my injuries heal correctly? Can I get compensation for missed work? If I have been in a car wreck, will I be compensated for damage to my vehicle? Do I need to see a doctor right away, or can I wait to see how I feel first? Do I need to hire a lawyer?

This book answers those questions and guides you through what you should do to win your injury case.

Personal Injury Myths:

If I contact the insurer I will receive a reasonable settlement offer.

When I have been an accident, the legal system is a way to get rich.

All lawyers who advertise for personal injury cases have the same experience and ability.

If I am in an accident and the other person's insurance company requests a recorded statement, I must give one or they will not settle my case.

The insurance adjuster is my friend.

The main goal of the insurance company is to pay me fair compensation as soon as possible.

Texas juries are generous.

Personal Injury Reality

In theory, insurance provides a valuable service by spreading the risk we all face that we will be in an accident and incur expenses that we could not afford on our own. Insurance is a way for many people to pool their money to protect against the chance of one person (or a few people) incurring a large financial loss. In a perfect world, when you are injured in an accident, the insurance company would pay you a prompt, fair settlement for your injuries.

Unfortunately, the reality is usually different. Insurance is a business like any other. Their goal is to make a profit. The more premiums they collect, and the less they pay out in claims, the more money they make. This profit motive causes the insurance company to work very hard to pay you as little as possible (or nothing) for your injuries.

The insurance company (even your own insurance) is not your friend. They make money by collecting and investing premiums, not by paying claims. And, when you have been hurt by someone else, and you are trying to get the other person's insurance to pay for your injuries, the insurance company will fight you even harder. The insurance adjuster may discourage you from talking with an attorney. The adjuster may ask you to give a recorded statement, where you might say something that would damage your case. Keep in mind that the insurance industry has spent many years and vast sums of money on two projects. First, they have conducted a vast public relations campaign to convince the public (from which juries are drawn) that most personal injury claims are bogus.

Second, insurance companies have spent a fortune and many years convincing lawmakers around the country to change the law to reduce or eliminate your ability to go to court to recover compensation when you are severely injured. Since the insurance industry is one of the richest in the country, and since it donates large sums of cash to political campaigns, the industry has been very effective in getting politicians to vote in favor of this so-called "tort reform" at the expense of the individual. Simply put, money talks, especially in politics.

As you fight the insurance company, trying to get them to pay for your injuries, you may have medical bills piling up. The insurance of the other person who injured you in your accident is usually under no obligation to pay your medical bills as they are incurred. This can cause severe financial hardship for many accident victims. This is one reason why it is important in serious accident cases to discuss your claim with an attorney as soon as possible. The attorney can evaluate your claim to determine if someone else was legally at fault, find out if there is insurance available to help pay for your injuries, and discover if there are any legal deadlines that must be met in order to avoid losing your ability to file suit on your claim.

How Insurance Companies Operate

All insurance companies employ very experienced defense attorneys, who sole responsibility is to protect the financial interests of the insurance company. Insurance companies are mainly in business to make money, not to pay claims. The less they pay out in accident claims, the greater their profit.

Insurance adjusters are trained to take advantage of the lack of knowledge most claimants have about their legal rights and the value of their accident claim. The adjuster may seem like a nice person who is friendly and pleasant over the phone and seems concerned with your welfare. However, never forget that their primary job is to protect the insurance company. The way they protect the insurance company is by finding a way to not give you any money, or if they have to pay you money they want to make sure they pay you as little as possible in order to resolve the matter and make it go away.

When you talk to the adjuster, he or she may try to get you to minimize the impact or extent of your injuries, or to get you to accept some responsibility for the accident that was really not your fault. They may also tell you how difficult it would be for you win your case in court. These are all standard tricks of the insurance adjuster, and ones that an experienced attorney can help you avoid.

What You Should Do After an Accident

First, do not make a statement to the insurance adjuster and do not let anyone pressure you, threaten you, or intimidate you into making a quick decision or signing any type of document. It is very common for insurance adjuster to try to get you to sign away your rights quickly. If you do this, you will regret it later.

Second, document your injuries and the accident itself. Gather all medical records, accident reports, witness statements and contact information in a folder. Take photographs of the accident scene and your injuries as soon as possible and keep them with your file. As the old saying goes "a picture is worth a thousand words", documenting your claim with photographs is worth thousands of dollars in helping you win a fair settlement or verdict for your accident.

Third, get to a physician to diagnose and treat your injuries as soon as possible. This provides crucial documentation of your injuries and gives you the best chance of making a full recovery.

Fourth, discuss your case with a personal injury attorney to evaluate the strengths and weaknesses of your claim and discover any legal deadlines that apply to your case. Delaying this step can permanently damage your claim. You should expect your lawyer to be completely honest with you. You lawyer expects the same honesty from you. When you meet with the attorney tell them everything about what happened in your accident and also let them know about any previous injuries you have had or lawsuits you have been involved with. If there is anything about your accident or your background that you are not sure is relevant to your claim, it probably is! You should feel safe confiding in your attorney, even regarding things that are personal or embarrassing. Usually everything you tell the lawyer is privileged attorney-client communication and cannot be revealed by the attorney without your permission or used against you. If you are not sure if something you want to tell the lawyer is privileged then ask. Being honest with your lawyer will avoid later surprises that may ruin your case.

Why You Should Hire an Attorney

Why do you think insurance companies discourage injury victims from hiring an attorney? They are not doing it to help you. They are doing it to help their bottom line.

The Insurance Research Council conducted a study that found that injury victims that use lawyers in personal injury claims receive more money than those who do not use a lawyer, even after the attorney's fees are paid!

Insurance companies do not want you to hire a lawyer because they know they will end up paying more money for your claim. Insurers make profits by collecting premiums, not by paying claims. The less they pay you, the more profit they make. Insurance adjusters are not promoted or rewarded for paying out more money than they have to in claims, but for paying out less.

Many people every year do nothing, or accept much less money than they should, regarding their injury claim. Usually this is because these people do not know what to do after they have been injured, or they believe that what they receive is all the money they can get. Many times, these injury victims feel confused or afraid. Do not let this happen to you. When you have been injured, doing nothing is the worst thing you can do.

What must be proven to win your case?

Just because you are injured does not mean that someone else must compensate you for your injuries. Some accidents are just unfortunate events where no one was at fault. Unless someone else's carelessness, or "negligence", caused your injuries, you do not have a viable case. Even if someone else's carelessness did cause your injury, under certain circumstances you still may not be able to sue them.

You must also understand that in Texas the law of "comparative negligence" controls how much money, if any, you can recover from someone who causes your injury. If the jury finds that you were partially at fault for the accident, they will reduce the amount you recover by the amount you were at fault. If the jury finds you were more than half at fault for your injuries, you will recover nothing.

For example, if your damages total $100,000.00 and if a jury awards you that amount but determines that you were 20% at fault, your $100,000.00 would be reduced by 20%, or $20,000.00, leaving you with $80,000.00. If the jury finds that you were 51% or more at fault in your accident, you will recover nothing. It may not seem fair, but it is the law in Texas. After we evaluate your case we will discuss with you the issue of comparative negligence to determine whether or not you have a case worth pursuing.

The Steps in a Personal Injury Claim

While every case is different, and not all cases require each of the steps outlined below, this is a list of the normal steps taken by personal injury attorneys in pursuing a claim.

Evaluate the client's claim, educate the client regarding the legal process for personal injury cases and determine any deadlines that apply.

Contact the opposing party's insurance company, giving them notice of the claim.

Gather evidence, including police accident reports, medical treatment and billing records, witness statements, etc.

Interview witnesses.

Analyze legal issues related to the case, including comparative negligence and any damage limits that may apply.

Review medical records and discuss the injuries and prognosis with the client's physicians.

We find out, by reviewing the client's insurance policies and contacting all medical providers, whether there are any liens that must be repaid by the client out of any settlement or verdict.

We decide whether settlement negotiations should be pursued or if suit should be filed in the case.

If a lawsuit is filed, prepare the witnesses, the client and the health-care providers for depositions and possible trial testimony.

Send and respond to "discovery" (formal, written questions and requests for documents) from the opposing party.

Conduct any depositions (formal, sworn, transcribed questioning of opposing party).

Attend mediation and attempt to settle the case short of trial.

Try the case.

Review the verdict to see if either party has grounds for appeal.

How to Choose an Injury Lawyer

Ask any attorney you are considering hiring for your injury case the following questions. If the attorney you are interviewing is missing these criteria or is evasive in answering these questions, you should leave their office immediately (or hang up the phone) and look elsewhere for your lawyer. Your claim is too important to spend any time with a lawyer who is not completely straightforward with you about themselves, your case or how the personal injury legal process works in Texas.

The lawyer interview process is a two-way street. You are looking for the best fit of an attorney to represent you and the lawyer is looking to see if you are a client they want to represent. Do not be afraid to ask questions. A lawyer who is being straight with you will welcome your questions and answer them honestly and without hesitation since they indicate that you take your case seriously and that you have started educating yourself about the legal process.

Questions to Ask Before You Hire a Lawyer

"Who in your office will actually handle my injury case and what are their qualifications?"

This may be the most important question you can ask and one that most clients do not even know they should ask. Often the lawyer you first speak with will not actually handle your case or be your lawyer if the case goes to trial. If you like and are impressed with the lawyer you first meet about your case, it is a rude shock to find out you may never see that lawyer again, especially at your trial. Imagine choosing a doctor for surgery and learning the morning of your operation that his young associate will actually cut you open.

Some firms will describe this as a "team approach" to your case, but this is just another way of saying that you will be pawned off on a less experienced lawyer once you sign up. If the hotshot partner is what attracted you to the firm in the first place, why would you settle for anything less once you decide to let the firm handle your case? And if the young associate lawyer assigned to your case is so good, why aren't they working for themselves?

Also make sure you understand how you will be kept informed of your case's progress. The number one client complaint against lawyers is lack of communication. Nothing is more frustrating than placing your trust in a lawyer and then having no idea what is happening with your case.

"How many years have you been in practice?"

The answer to this question will tell you about the experience level of your lawyer. Also ask what specifically they have done during those years of practice. Being listed on a personal injury lawyer "directory" often only requires a credit card and a pulse and does not necessarily mean that lawyer has the relevant experience to help you with your case. The same is true of Google search results on the internet. Just because someone paid an internet search optimization expert to get them to page one of Google search results does not mean they are the best attorney for your case.

Some lawyers get into personal injury work when their other practice areas dry up for some reason. Or they simply add personal injury to their list of practice areas in hopes of landing a big case while they pursue all their other practice areas that have nothing to do with personal injury work. Some of these lawyers may never have tried a case and even if they have, they may have only tried cases before a judge and never before a jury.

"How much experience do you have representing personal injury victims?"

Your attorney should have real experience developing, negotiating, mediating and (when necessary) trying personal injury cases. Personal injury law is too complicated to be entrusted to someone who "dabbles in personal injury". You do not want a lawyer who is a "jack of all trades and a master of none". You only get one shot to receive justice for your personal injury case and you want to work with a lawyer whose experience gives you the best chance of success.

"Have you ever been disciplined by the State Bar?"

A disciplinary history with the State Bar often indicates a lawyer who does not "take care of business" for his or her clients. The State Bar may discipline a lawyer for lying to a client or a judge, neglecting a case, accepting a case in an area in which they are incompetent or mishandling client money.

Sometimes a disciplinary history indicates a lawyer who has a problem with drugs or alcohol, emotional or psychological issues, financial pressures or simply a lack of professionalism. Regardless of the reason, do you really want a lawyer with these problems handling your injury case? At a minimum you have a right to know if the lawyer you are considering has ever been disciplined by the State Bar. You may verify whether a lawyer has ever been disciplined by the State Bar of Texas by calling (800) 204-2222 or looking online at the "Find a Lawyer" section of www.texasbar.com

"What are the potential costs for developing my case and how are you paid?"

Even though most personal injury cases are "contingency cases" (where the lawyer fronts the costs and is repaid these costs and receives his legal fee if he wins your case) it is important to understand the costs involved in pursuing the case and also how the money is divided if you win your case.

You should demand a simple, clear, written contract with your attorney that spells out exactly what costs you are responsible for and what the attorney will receive as their fee. The attorney should also give you their assessment of what the costs may be to develop the case and that must be reimbursed out of any recovery. That way there are no unpleasant surprises when the case settles or you win at trial.

"What challenges do you foresee in my case?"

One of the biggest responsibilities of your lawyer is to "step into the shoes" of the defense lawyer and try to find any weaknesses in your case that can be used against you. This is where experience really pays off because an experienced attorney can spot potential pitfalls and address them. There is no such thing as a perfect injury case and you do not want a lawyer that sugar-coats the truth. If the lawyer has serious doubts about your ability to win your case, you have a right to know that right up front. Your lawyer should give you their honest assessment of your claim, "warts and all", so that you can make smart choices.

"What will be the final outcome of my case?"

This is really a test to see if the lawyer is honest. The only acceptable answer is that the attorney can **NOT** promise a specific outcome. Any other response is unethical and dishonest and should cause you to hang up the phone or walk out of the lawyer's office immediately.

No lawyer can tell you with total certainty that an insurance company will offer a fair settlement before you have to file a lawsuit or before you go to trial. If you go to trial, remember that judges and juries are people and people are unpredictable so no attorney can honestly promise you what they will decide in the trial of a specific case. Any honest attorney will tell you that they have lost cases they felt they should have won, and won cases they felt they had should have lost. If not then they probably have not tried very many cases! Experience, preparation and creativity in presenting your case can help tilt the odds in your favor, but your attorney can only promise to do the very best they can to win your case.

Navigating the Lawyer Advertising Jungle

If you search the internet for "personal injury lawyer" you will be bombarded by advertisements for attorneys claiming that they handle injury cases. Many of these ads say the same things, such as "no fee if no recovery", "get the money you deserve", "aggressive trial lawyer" or "insurance companies fear us". They may even have a gimmick such as a photograph of a bulldog or a shark to show that they are tough.

What exactly does all this mean? How do you go about telling these attorneys apart? Most importantly, how do you choose the right attorney for your case?

When you see "no fee if no recovery" remember that you are almost always liable for your medical expenses regardless of how your case turns out. If you win enough money, that money can be used towards paying off those bills. However, if you lose, or do not recover enough money, you are still responsible for paying your own medical bills. Be sure and clarify exactly how any recovery is divided as well as what bills you are responsible for (no matter how the case turns out) with any attorney you are considering hiring.

Also remember that most health insurance policies including private insurance as well as Medicare and Medicaid allow your insurance company to take away money you obtain from the party that injured you in order to repay your insurer for money it spent on your injuries. This is known as "subrogation" and can be complicated. It is always a good idea to discuss subrogation with an attorney as early in your case as possible. Otherwise, you might receive a nasty surprise when your insurance company comes to take away your settlement money.

When you read such phrases as "get the money you deserve" be wary of any attorney that promises you that it will be easy to get you lots of money. Any attorney who promises you this is not telling you the truth because no one can predict exactly what will happen ahead of time in trying to either settle your case or take it to trial. Remember also that the evaluation of the case is an ongoing process. The prospects for a case may change as new facts are discovered during the investigation and preparation of your claim.

If the attorney advertisement states that he or she is an "aggressive trial lawyer" find out exactly what this means. Does the attorney actually take cases to trial, or does he settle most of them, or refer them out to other attorneys when cases need to go to trial? Also, what does "aggressive" mean? Every attorney should zealously represent their client, but if they are obnoxious to the opposing attorney or the insurance adjuster, or for that matter, the judge or jury, they may do more damage to your case than someone who treats everyone involved with courtesy and respect while still fighting hard for your rights.

Being effective is not the same as being rude. Remember, some jurors already have in their minds a stereotype of a personal injury trial lawyer (and often their client!) as greedy, obnoxious, dishonest and opportunistic. If your attorney's demeanor reinforces this stereotype, you may have a problem. If the jury does not like your attorney or does not believe your attorney, they will usually find a way to make sure you lose.

If an attorney claims that "insurance companies fear us" be careful. The reputation of your attorney is important in that insurance companies respect attorneys that thoroughly prepare and are willing to take cases to trial. However, remember that insurance companies also have excellent attorneys, and these insurers deal with claims like yours all the time. Thanks to the successful insurance industry public relations media campaign that has convinced many potential jurors that all personal injury plaintiffs are out to "get rich quick" with a frivolous lawsuit, insurers are often willing to "roll the dice" by taking a case to trial regardless of who the attorney for the plaintiff is. Sometimes this is done as a matter of policy to establish the insurance company as being tough on all claims and scare away potential litigants. Therefore, it is important to have an attorney that is willing and able to take your case to trial when necessary.

Other Things to Watch Out For

It is important to remember a few other things when looking at attorney advertising. First, remember that anyone can create a website. A slick internet website does not necessarily mean that the attorney is the right one for you, or even a very good attorney. It is important that you check out the lawyer's credentials and talk with them about how they will approach your case before you decide to hire them. Ask the lawyer if they offer a written guide like this one with information about their methods for handling cases and their experience and qualifications.

You should be wary of any attorney that pressures you to sign a contract quickly. Remember that attorneys that sign up too many cases may not have the time and resources to properly prepare your case. Also, you should be given time to review the contract in a relaxed setting, and have all your questions answered, before you make the decision to hire an attorney.

Avoid any attorney who contacts you first, trying to get you to hire him for your particular claim (and report them to the State Bar of Texas and the police). Texas has strict rules regarding attorneys, or anyone working on behalf of an attorney (called "runners") who solicit clients after an accident either by telephone, in person (on the street or in the hospital, for example) or in writing (except under limited circumstances). Lawyers who violate these rules can lose their license and go to jail. You should beware of attorneys who engage in such obnoxious (and illegal) practices.

Make sure that the lawyer is not running his or her practice as a "settlement mill" that takes way too many cases, hoping to settle them all, and then, if cases need to go to trial, farms them out to other attorneys. They may also be under pressure to pay off all the expensive advertising that got clients to call and therefore pressure you to accept a "lowball" offer just to get some money out of the case quickly.

The attorney should be able to explain to you, clearly and concisely, how the personal injury claims process works. They should also be able to explain to you the procedure if your case goes to trial. Personal injury cases, and truck accidents in particular, are subject to unique laws, regulations and potential pitfalls. Therefore, it is important to find an attorney that deals with automobile accident cases on a regular basis and who is willing to take them trial when necessary. Understand that the insurance company on the other side knows which attorneys go to trial and which attorneys settle everything, and this affects their thinking as they evaluate whether to settle your case and for how much.

Make sure you are comfortable with the lawyer's personality since you are going to be working together for a while. To be successful in resolving your claim it is important for you and your attorney to work as a team.

Wrapping up

Congratulations! Having read this guide, you now know much more than most injury victims about how to protect your rights and win your Texas injury case. If you have questions or need help, contact us at the Todd Law Firm for a free case evaluation.

About David Todd

Personal injury lawyer David Todd has helped injury victims obtain justice throughout Texas since 1989. He a Texas Super Lawyer and is Board Certified in Family Law by the Texas Board of Legal Specialization. For more information and a free case evaluation call (512) 472-7799 or visit us on the web at davidtoddlaw.com.

David Todd, Attorney at Law
Todd Law Firm
3800 N. Lamar Blvd., Ste. 200
Austin, TX 78756
(512) 472-7799
davidtoddlaw.com